VOLCANOES
and Earthquakes

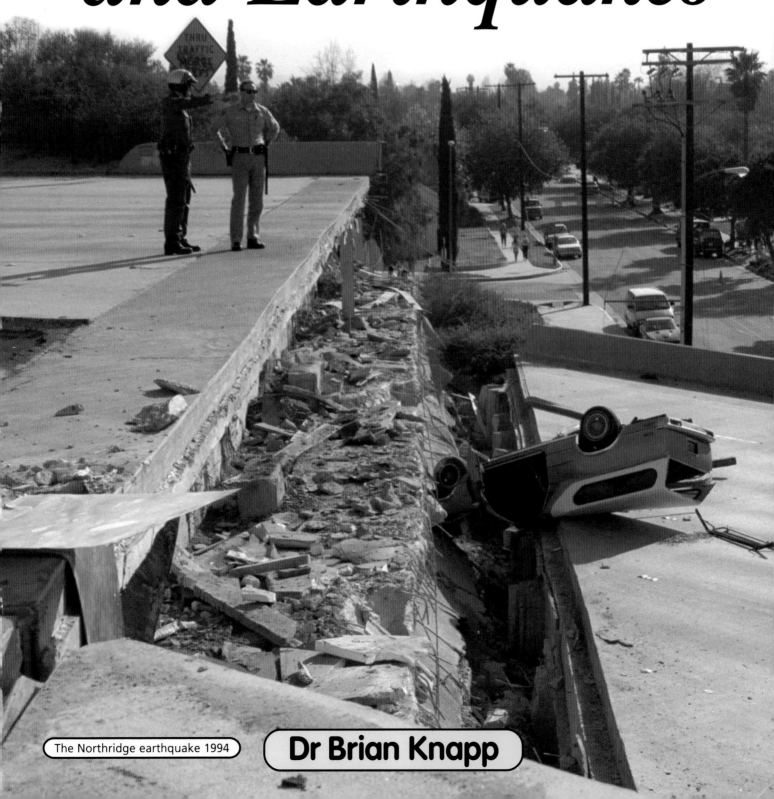

The Northridge earthquake 1994

Dr Brian Knapp

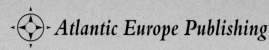

Atlantic Europe Publishing

First published in 2003 by
Atlantic Europe Publishing Company Ltd

Copyright © 2003
Atlantic Europe Publishing Company Ltd

Author
Brian Knapp, BSc, PhD
Art Director
Duncan McCrae, BSc
Senior Designer
Adele Humphries, BA, PGCE
Editors
Lisa Magloff, BA, and *Gillian Gatehouse*
Illustrations by
David Woodroffe, except *David Hardy* (page 34)
and *Simon Tegg* (pages 36–37)
Scans by
Earthscape Editions and *Global Graphics sro*
Designed and produced by
Earthscape Editions
Printed in Hong Kong by
Wing King Tong Company Ltd

Volcanoes and Earthquakes
– *Curriculum Visions*
**A CIP record for this book is available from
the British Library**

Paperback ISBN 1-86214-324-2
Hardback ISBN 1-86214-326-9

*This product is manufactured from sustainable
managed forests. For every tree cut down at least one
more is planted.*

Spirit Lake and Mt St Helens crater

Curriculum Visions

Curriculum Visions is a registered trademark of
Atlantic Europe Publishing Company Ltd.

Glossary
There is a glossary on pages 46–47.
Glossary terms are referred to in the
text by using CAPITALS.

Index
There is an index on page 48.

Teacher's Guide
There is a Teacher's Guide to
accompany this book, available
only from the publisher.

Posters
Two posters showing the key features of
volcanoes and earthquakes are available
as part of a package only from the publisher.

Dedicated Web Site
There's more about other great Curriculum
Visions packs and a wealth of supporting
information available at our dedicated web site:

www.CurriculumVisions.com/volcano

Picture credits
All photographs are from the Earthscape Editions
photolibrary except the following:
(c=centre t=top b=bottom l=left r=right)
FEMA 1, 29tl, 29c inset, 29br, 40bl, 40br, 41t; *W. Millan*
43 all photos; *NASA* 37tr; *Keith Ronnholm* 6b, 15cr;
USGS COVER (Griggs, J.D.), 3 (Decker, R.), 4, 7b,
8–9 (Griggs J.D.), 13c (Griggs J.D.), 15tr (Casadevall,
T.J.), 17tl (Austin Post), 17cl (Casadevall, T.J.), 19tr
(Griggs, J.D.), 28t, 31bl, 39tl, 39tr (Griggs, J.D.),
39ctr (Casadevall, T.J.), 45br; *USGS/HVO* 39ctl;
G. Wadge/NERC 45tr.

Contents

Lava fountain in Hawaii

Volcanoes and earthquakes

These are the *natural* features you might expect to see in a volcanic landscape.

1 A **VOLCANO** is a special type of mountain which periodically sends out, or erupts, liquid material from within the Earth. See examples of types of **ERUPTIONS** on pages 6 to 9.

2 The molten rock that makes all volcanoes begins deep underground, where it is called **MAGMA**. A more detailed description is on page 10.

3 Many volcanoes build **CONES**, which make volcanic mountains if they get big enough. See the inside of a volcano, its supply pipe, or **VENT**, and its **CRATER** on pages 12 to 13.

4 The molten rock may come out at the surface in the form of a giant explosion. Find out about this on page 14.

5 Sometimes ash and gases shoot out sideways from a volcano to give **GLOWING AVALANCHES**. More information on these can be found on page 15.

6 Explosive eruptions produce **ASH**, cinders, and even **VOLCANIC BOMBS**, as described on pages 16 to 17.

7 When liquid rock, or **LAVA**, flows across the ground it cools and quickly solidifies as shown on page 19.

8 Some magma pushes its way between layers of rock and makes new sheets of volcanic rock called **SILLS**, or **DYKES**. When the rock of the magma chamber cools it

Extinct

Active

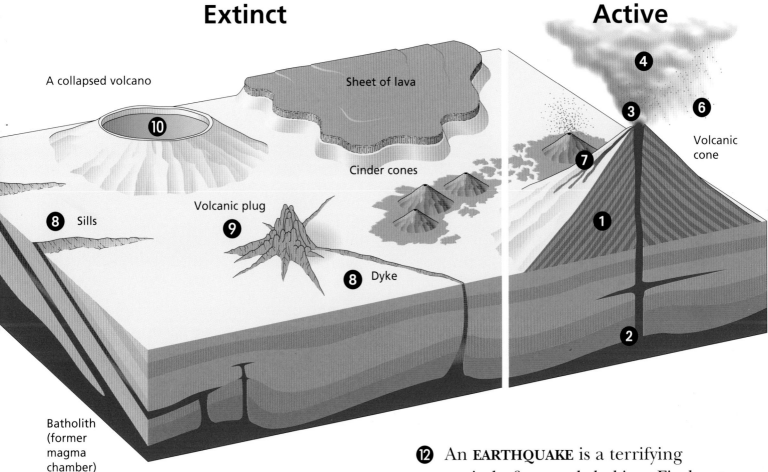

A collapsed volcano

Sheet of lava

Cinder cones

Volcanic plug

⑧ Sills

⑨

⑧ Dyke

Batholith
(former
magma
chamber)

⑩

④

③

⑥

Volcanic
cone

⑦

①

②

forms a **BATHOLITH**. See what features result on pages 20 to 21.

❾ When volcanoes cease erupting for good, their cones are eventually eroded away. See what features the volcanic **PLUG** of an ancient vent makes on pages 22 to 23.

❿ Sometimes the entire top of a volcano collapses to form a pit called a **CALDERA** which then fills with water to give a **CRATER LAKE**. See this on pages 24 to 25.

⓫ The hot rocks remaining underground may turn ground water into steam and make a **GEYSER**. Find out what this is like on pages 26 to 27.

⓬ An **EARTHQUAKE** is a terrifying period of ground shaking. Find out what happens on pages 28 to 29.

⓭ Earthquakes are caused by slabs of the Earth's **CRUST** slipping past one another. See the **SHOCK WAVES** they produce on page 30.

⓮ Earthquake patterns and their energy can be measured. Information on this is on pages 32 to 33.

⓯ Earthquakes and volcanoes occur at the boundaries of the Earth's great crustal **PLATES**. More information on these is on pages 34 to 37.

⓰ Both volcanoes and earthquakes cause **DISASTERS**. Look at several examples to see how disasters can be dealt with and predicted on pages 38 to 45.

A volcano explodes

A volcanic eruption can be one of the most frightening experiences on Earth because of the violence with which some eruptions begin.

It was 8.32 a.m. on a glorious sunny morning in May 1980. There wasn't a cloud in the sky to spoil the view of Mt St Helens, a peak in the forest wilderness of the Cascade Mountains of the United States. Campers on vacation could see the forests on the lower flanks of the mountain and above them a summit capped by snowfields and a glacier.

Mt St Helens is, however, no ordinary mountain. It is a **VOLCANO**.

As people ate their breakfast and looked at the mountain, the **ERUPTION** began. Quite suddenly, part of the summit of Mt St Helens fell away, and a dense grey cloud of fiery gas and **ASH** started racing towards them at the speed of an express train (picture ①).

For a few seconds the campers were stunned at the violence of this natural

▼ ① Probably the most stunning view that you can see on Earth is an explosive eruption in progress. This view was taken during the first minute of an eruption, looking at the side of the mountain that was blasted away.

explosion. Then they got into their cars and fled for their lives as the cloud bore down on them.

They had just minutes to try to outrun the volcano. Some made it, some did not (picture ②).

At 8.32 a.m. Mt St Helens had exploded with tremendous violence and devastating results, blowing part of its side right away and flattening a vast area of forest (picture ③).

▲ ② This car belonged to some people who did not manage to escape. The car was crushed by the force of the gases and ash in the exploding volcano.

▼ ③ This picture was taken from high above the volcano after the eruption had ended. The picture looks straight down on the volcano and sets out the scene just like a map. The green area on the left is untouched forest. The grey area on the right has no forest left, just bare soil. The right-hand side of the volcano has been blown away.

The volcano as seen from above.

Mt St Helens
USA

The side of the volcano has blown away.

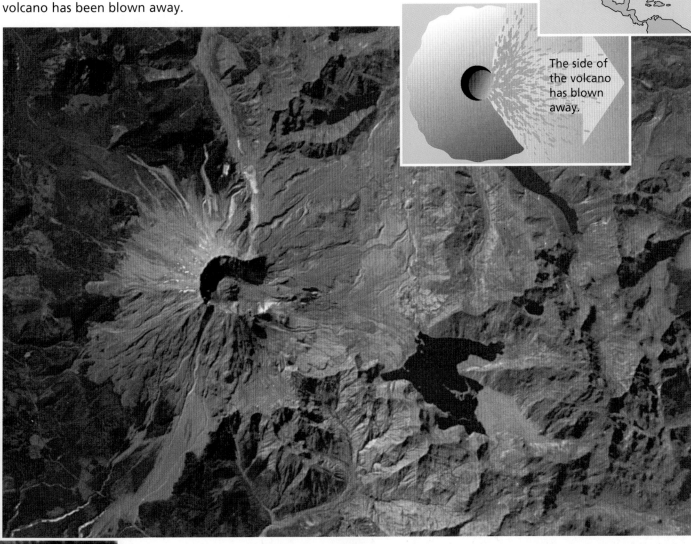

A fountain of fire

Not all volcanoes erupt explosively. Those that erupt frequently tend to produce 'fountains' and 'rivers' of molten rock instead.

Mt St Helens (shown on page 6) was a very dangerous volcano to be near. But not all volcanoes are like this. Picture ① shows the top of the volcano Kilauea, on the island of Hawaii, in the Pacific Ocean (picture ②). It is one of the biggest and most **ACTIVE VOLCANOES** in the world.

From the summit of Kilauea, fountains of **MOLTEN** rock, called LAVA, shoot hundreds of metres up into the air, then fall to the ground, forming natural rivers at 1,000°C. There is no major explosion, simply long rivers of lava (picture ③).

▶ ① Scientists can look at Kilauea volcano in Hawaii even while it erupts. That is because it erupts with little violence. Here you see a fountain of molten rock rising from the **CRATER.** Notice that the erupting lava is red hot, but that it quickly changes colour as it cools and turns black. Some cooling even occurs while the fountain of molten rock is in the air.

Why are volcanoes so different?

The volcanoes shown on this page and on page 6 are both erupting. But the way they erupt and the danger to people couldn't be more different. So what is it that makes each volcano behave differently? To find out the answer to this, we have to know how volcanoes work. That is what we will see on the following pages.

▶ ② The location of Kilauea.

Hawaii
Kilauea ●

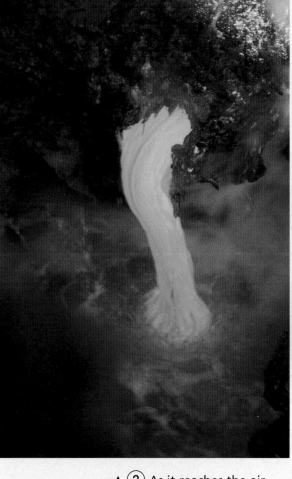

▲ ③ As it reaches the air, the yellow molten rock **CONGEALS** and forms a black rock that looks like tar. Molten lava flows underneath the black crust.

Where molten rock comes from

Molten rock surges up from underground chambers through weaknesses in the ground. The molten rock is called magma.

All of the very different events that we have seen on the previous pages – the flowing rock, the explosions, and the gases and dust thrown high into the air – have a single source: the molten rock that surges from deep underground.

Magma and magma chambers

The molten rock that supplies a volcano is called MAGMA. The place where the magma is stored is called a MAGMA CHAMBER (picture ①).

▼ ① Hot molten rock is lighter than cold rock, so it begins to rise (A). The molten rock does this by melting the solid rock roof above. In this way the molten rock rises like a hot air balloon, but incredibly slowly, in some cases taking millions of years to get close to the surface (B). When the magma gets close enough to the surface, the rocks above become cracked and weak. Molten rock can then punch up through the weak areas to form volcanoes (C).

The word 'magma' comes from the Greek word for dough, which is another slightly sticky mixture, full of trapped gas bubbles that expand and then rise as it cools.

Molten rock is often over 1,000°C and is under tremendous pressure.

To understand what is happening, think of a volcano as a kind of rocket turned upside down.

A rocket stores its fuel as liquids under pressure in big tanks, or chambers. These liquids feed through pipes where they turn into immensely hot gases.

A volcano stores its liquid fuel in vast, underground magma chambers. Each chamber may be tens of kilometres across and more than a kilometre deep.

A

B

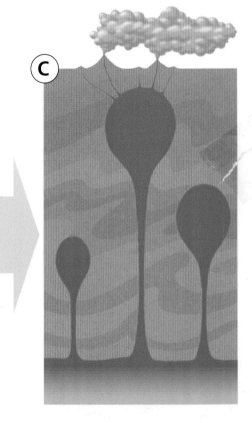

C

Finding a way to the surface

The magma has to find a way to the surface before an eruption can occur. It begins as molten rock tens of kilometres below the surface in a part of the Earth called the **MANTLE**. It then has to rise through the cold, hard rocks of the outer layer, called the **CRUST** (picture ②). If the rocks are thick and tough, the molten rock never reaches the surface and eventually cools into the **IGNEOUS ROCK** we know as **GRANITE**.

But where the rocks above are weak and cracked, they provide a route for the magma to escape.

There are three kinds of places where the Earth's surface is very weak:

▶ where the Earth's crust is pulling apart,
▶ where it is squeezing together, and
▶ where it is thin.

Above each place we find volcanoes.

Fissures and pipes

Where the Earth's rocks are squeezing together, the rock is thick. Magma has to 'punch' and melt its way to the surface, rising through a 'chimney' and finally erupting with great violence. This is the kind of thing that happened at Mt St Helens (see page 6).

Where the Earth's rocks are pulling apart, or the crust is thin, great cracks or **FISSURES** appear, making it easy for magma to rise to the surface and flood across the land or sea bed as lava. Because it doesn't need to punch its way up, the eruption is much less violent, as was the case at Kilauea, Hawaii (see page 8).

▶ ② The surface of the Earth is made of hard, cold rocks. But it is only a thin layer compared to the thickness of the Earth. We call it the crust. Below it is a much thicker layer that is very hot. It is called the mantle. From time to time parts of this layer melt. Between the mantle and the centre of the Earth lies the **CORE**.

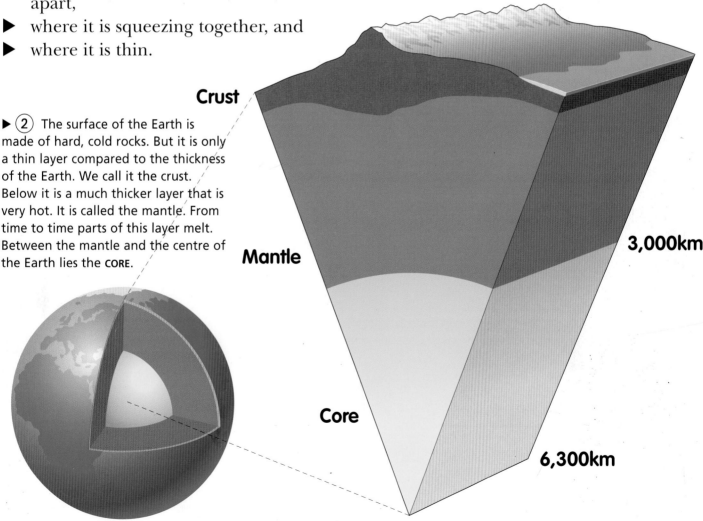

Crust

Mantle

Core

3,000km

6,300km

Weblink:www.CurriculumVisions.com/volcano

Volcanic mountains

When magma erupts from a vent, it often builds up into a mountain shaped like a cone. At the top of the cone lies a crater.

Volcanoes are places where magma (molten rock) flows out of or explodes from the ground. Volcanoes may erupt periodically over thousands of years and in this way build up a volcanic mountain (picture ①).

▼ ① This diagram shows the main features of a volcano and how it is connected to the magma chamber below. Notice that there are many lines of weakness above the magma chamber. If more than one weakness is opened up, then several volcanoes can erupt side by side. Sometimes small vents open on the flanks of the volcano. When this happens, small cones build and the main volcano loses its balanced shape.

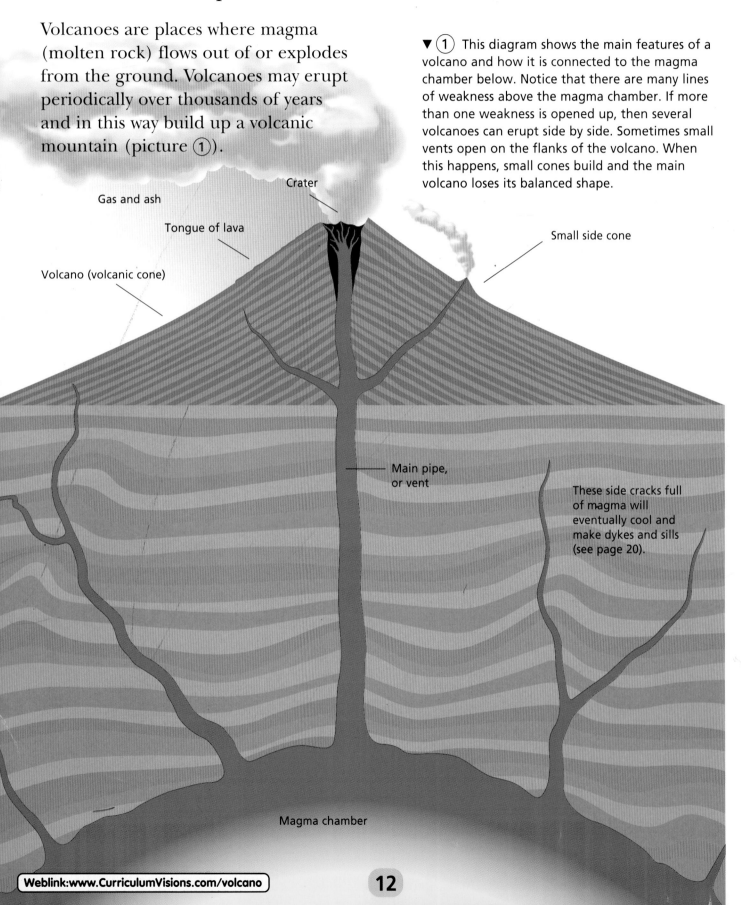

Gas and ash

Crater

Tongue of lava

Small side cone

Volcano (volcanic cone)

Main pipe, or vent

These side cracks full of magma will eventually cool and make dykes and sills (see page 20).

Magma chamber

Vent and crater

Volcanic eruptions produce all kinds of landscapes, but many volcanoes are conical mountains with a pit in the top, called a **CRATER** (picture ②).

A volcano of this kind is fed by a great, circular chimney, called a **VENT**. As the erupting volcano throws out, or ejects, material, it builds up a cone around itself. The vent gets taller and taller as the cone grows higher and higher.

▼ ② The crater area at the top of a volcano.

Layers

Mountains of layers

Volcanic mountains are built from the materials they spew out during eruptions.

If lava is to help build a mountain and not run off across a nearby plain, then it has to move quite slowly, and cool while still near to the crater. The lava that produces cones therefore has to be 'sticky' lava.

Few mountains are made entirely of lava. Normally they are also made of layers of fine rock fragments. Most explosive eruptions send great volumes of rock fragments, such as fine ash, high into the sky. Some of it lands back on the volcano.

In this way, each eruption may create a layer of ash and a few tongues of lava to add to the mountain. Over thousands of years such a process can build mountains thousands of metres high.

Weblink:www.CurriculumVisions.com/volcano

Explosive eruptions

Some volcanoes erupt explosively. They are mainly volcanoes that erupt ash rather than lava.

As we saw on page 6, some volcanoes erupt violently with massive explosions. They are volcanoes that have long, quiet periods between eruptions.

In general, the longer the time between eruptions, the more violent and explosive the eruption, and the steeper the sides of the volcano tend to be. Thus, steep-sided volcanoes are the most dangerous kind to be near.

Volcanoes stop and start

Most volcanoes go through a cycle of events, with eruption followed by a quiet spell (picture ①).

When a volcano erupts, it does so because the pressure in the full magma chamber below is so great that magma can force its way to the surface.

At first, the eruption throws out ash and fragments of rock, and then it sends tongues of lava from its crater.

Eventually, however, there is no longer enough pressure to push magma up the vent, and so the magma stops rising to the surface.

It may take anything from a few days to a few months for this to happen. Finally, the last of the magma starts to cool in the vent, and that plugs the volcano and it gets quiet again.

Dormant means danger

While a volcano is refilling its magma chamber, it is said to be **DORMANT** (sleeping). The longer the time it takes for the magma chamber to fill, the longer the remains of the old rock have to cool in the vent, and the thicker the plug.

▼ ① The cycle of eruption

Active

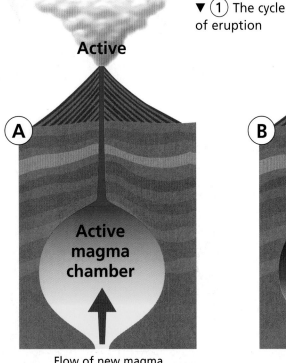

(A)

Active magma chamber

Flow of new magma

Dormant

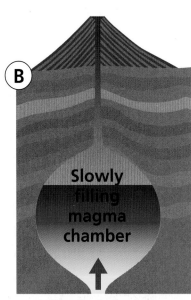

(B)

Slowly filling magma chamber

Slow flow of magma

Extinct

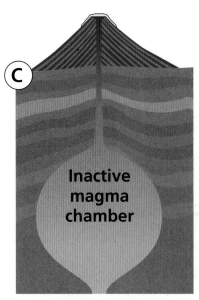

(C)

Inactive magma chamber

Magma solidified

◀▼ ② This is a volcano that erupts sticky lava (left). Each explosion has to break up a thick plug of rock, and so the explosion is very violent. This is like the volcano Pinatubo in the Philippines (below).

So the longer a volcano is dormant, the greater the pressure that will be needed in the magma chamber to blow out the plug.

As you can see, a volcano that doesn't erupt very often is always likely to erupt very explosively as it clears its vent of the thick plug of old magma (picture ②).

Every so often, the plug of rock is stuck so firmly in the old vent that it simply cannot be blown away (picture ③). In this case, the pressure of the magma below the volcano will cause **EARTHQUAKES** and they will weaken the rock above. Then the volcano will find a new route to the surface, often through the weakened side of the mountain. When this happens, the blast will not be straight up but sideways over the surrounding landscape. This produces a **GLOWING AVALANCHE** of gases and ash that rushes across the surrounding landscape. (Mt St Helens blew up like this after more than a century of being dormant, see page 6.)

▲▼ ③ This is a volcano where the plug is stuck fast (below), and the volcano erupts from a new opening on the side of the mountain. This is like the volcano Mt St Helens in the United States (above).

Ash, cinders and bombs

An explosion throws huge volumes of gas and a great spray of tiny pieces of magma high into the air. These pieces cool and form a white powder or dust, called ash, or brown bubbly stone, called cinders or bombs.

Magma is liquid rock. But dissolved in the molten rock is a large amount of gas under pressure. Most of the violent effects of the volcano come from the way that the gases escape from the magma and expand as they escape from the crater (picture ①).

Volcanic clouds

When a volcano explodes violently, the most dramatic sight is the tall, billowing cloud that rises from the mountain summit.

This cloud is made of many things. First, it contains invisible gases. They include water vapour and carbon dioxide.

The cloud also contains ash. This fine, powdery dust gets caught up in the blast of gas from the volcano and is thrown high into the air. That is partly what makes the cloud visible (picture ②).

As the water vapour cools in the air, it turns to droplets. That is what gives shape to the huge thundercloud that develops over an erupting volcano.

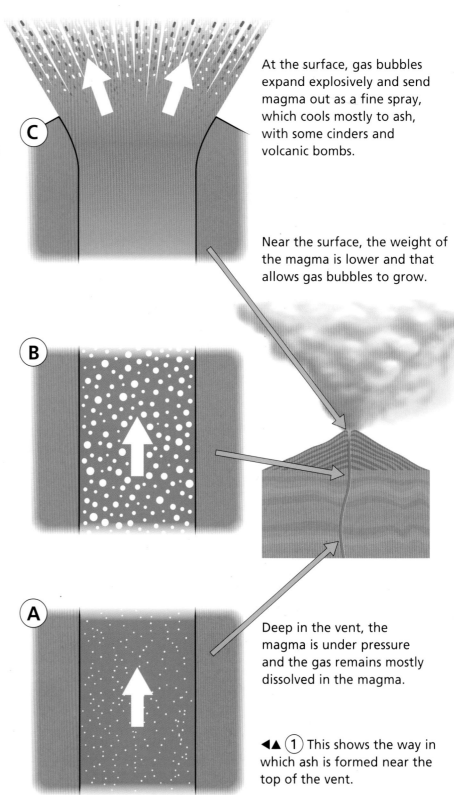

At the surface, gas bubbles expand explosively and send magma out as a fine spray, which cools mostly to ash, with some cinders and volcanic bombs.

Near the surface, the weight of the magma is lower and that allows gas bubbles to grow.

Deep in the vent, the magma is under pressure and the gas remains mostly dissolved in the magma.

◄▲ ① This shows the way in which ash is formed near the top of the vent.

◄ ② Here you can see the cloud of gases and ash that erupted from Mt St Helens in 1980. You can see ash falling back onto the cone to the left of the crater. Notice also the thundercloud in the background.

▲ ③ Ash

Ash, cinders and bombs

Ash begins as molten magma. Picture ① shows how, as the magma rises up the vent, the pressure gets smaller and the gas bubbles in the magma grow so fast that they eventually rip the magma apart. The spray of rock fragments is then carried up with the gases, where they cool into small pieces of rock. The finest dust (which makes up the majority of the material) is the ash (picture ③). Pea to golf-ball-sized pieces are called cinders. The largest fragments are called **VOLCANIC BOMBS** (picture ④).

▲► ④ The large piece is a volcanic bomb that weighs about 500g. See how it is partly moulded from its travel through the air. The smaller pieces are cinders. Each weighs about 20g. Notice that the marks on the surface show where gas bubbles in the molten rock have burst.

Lava

As soon as lava leaves the vent, it begins to cool and turn into rock. When lava cools, its surface can be smooth or it can break up into rough boulders.

No matter how sticky or runny the lava is while it is molten, eventually it will cool and become solid rock (picture ①).

▼ ① In this picture lava is pouring into the sea and being cooled by the water. Notice the treacly nature of the lava. The surface skin has become solid and turned black. The red molten lava still oozes out from below.

▲ ② Lava tends to be very sticky or very runny. On the left is sticky lava, called aa lava. It is so sticky that it moves very slowly. That gives the surface time to cool. Once cooled, the surface becomes brittle and is broken up as it is carried along by the flowing lava below. Aa lava makes a rough, bouldery type of surface. The picture on the right is runny, or pahoehoe, lava. It only forms a thin skin and is smooth.

As the lava changes from red to black, it develops a skin (picture ②). Look carefully at the surface of the 'skin' on the lava flow and compare it with the solid rock shown in the picture.

Lava exposed to the air for a long time turns brown (it contains a lot of iron and so has 'rusted'). But otherwise the surface shapes are very similar.

Names for lava

The Hawaiian islanders in the Pacific Ocean have the world's biggest volcano (Mauna Loa), and the names of volcanic rock are taken from the Hawaiian language (pictures ② and ③). Lava with a smooth surface is called **PAHOEHOE LAVA** (pronounced *pa-howie-howie*). Lava with a rough, broken surface is **AA LAVA** (pronounced *aaah, aaah*).

In general, the stickier the lava, the rougher the surface it produces.

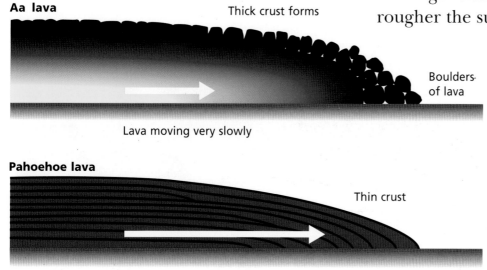

Aa lava

Thick crust forms

Boulders of lava

Lava moving very slowly

Pahoehoe lava

Thin crust

Lava moving fairly quickly

◄ ③ This diagram shows a side view through the lava. The sticky lava is thick and develops a crust that breaks up as the lava below moves; the more runny lava moves forwards in thin sheets and cools all at the same time.

Dykes, sills and batholiths

There are many new features produced inside an active volcano and on the rocks on which it is built. Dykes, sills, plugs and batholiths are names of volcanic features that are only seen when the volcano is worn away.

As a magma chamber grows, it presses on the rocks above and tends to push them up in an arch, cracking the rocks or prising one rock layer from another. These lines of weakness can provide underground routes for magma to follow.

Dykes and sills

Lines of weakness that reach the surface make volcanic cones. But many cracks stay entirely under the ground. If magma flows into these cracks it can form a sheet of material that later cools into tough rock. A sheet of rock that follows cracks upwards, cutting through other layers of rock, is called a **DYKE** (picture ①). You can remember a dyke as an upright sheet with 'walls'.

Magma can also force its way between layers of rock and make a new rock layer. This is called a **SILL** (picture ②). You can remember a sill as having a 'roof' and a 'floor'. Dykes and sills can be quite common (picture ③).

At the end of an eruption, even the cracks leading to the surface fill with magma that then cools. Magma cooling in the vent of a volcano makes a massive **PLUG** (see page 22).

Batholiths

As a volcano becomes extinct, the magma chamber also cools and eventually turns into rock (picture ④).

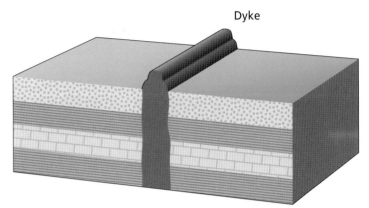

▲ ① A dyke was once a sheet of molten volcanic rock that cut its way *across* layers of rock. Because it is harder than the nearby rock, it has stood up to erosion and makes a ridge in the landscape.

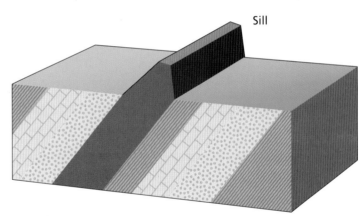

▲ ② A sill was once a sheet of molten volcanic rock that squeezed its way *between* layers of rock. Like a dyke, a sill is harder than the nearby rock. It has stood up to erosion and makes a ridge in the landscape.

It is called a **BATHOLITH**. Batholiths are huge. Dartmoor is a small example. Many of them make impressive scenery. Batholiths, for example, make up much of the mountains of California (picture ⑤).

When the cooling takes a long time, the stone grows many big crystals. This type of rock is called **GRANITE**.

◀ ③ Dykes and sills are very common in western Scotland, Northern Ireland and Northern England. The main areas are marked in red. The picture far left shows Hadrian's wall, which is built on a sill.

▼▶ ④ Dartmoor, in southwest England, is an area of high granite moors. It was once the magma chamber of an ancient series of volcanoes. The diagram on the right shows how the volcanoes were worn away, exposing the tough rocks of the old magma chamber. Their toughness means that these rocks now make the highest land in the landscape.

Magma chamber

Erosion

Batholith

▶ ⑤ A granite batholith in California's Sierra Nevada Mountains.

Landscape of volcanic 'plumbing'

Volcanoes are dangerous when they are active. But long after they have become completely inactive, or **EXTINCT**, their tough rock often still makes impressive scenery.

That is because volcanic rock stands up well to the forces of the weather. So when a volcano becomes extinct, and the softer rocks of the cone are worn away (**ERODED**), it is these features of the underground 'plumbing' that remain behind.

Weblink:www.CurriculumVisions.com/volcano

Volcanic plugs

The plugs that fill vents are made of hard rock that often survive long after the rest of the volcano has been worn away.

Some of the toughest rocks are the plugs of old volcanoes. The softer rocks on the flanks of the volcano soon wear away once the volcano becomes extinct, leaving just the plug standing (picture ①).

In the past, this hard plug often made an ideal place for defence. In France there is an area, near the town of Le Puy, where there are many small plugs, each with a castle or church on it (picture ②).

The Edinburgh volcanoes

Edinburgh is a superb example of how extinct volcanoes can help shape a city.

Edinburgh Castle was built on a plug of volcanic rock that overlooks the Firth of Forth. The tall plug, with natural cliffs on three sides, made a superb defensive position against attack. On the east side there is a natural ramp of rocks. This narrow and easily defended 'causeway'

makes it easy to get from the castle to the lower land.

The oldest part of the city (now called the Old Town) was built on the causeway, its tall, cramped buildings lining the roads that make up the Royal Mile. Other volcanic plugs right in the city centre provide more hills from which there are splendid views.

The Royal Mile leads to Holyrood House. Here there are more volcanic features. The high cliff called Salisbury Crags is a sill, and the summit of the hill is Arthur's Seat, the site of another ancient volcano (picture ③).

▼ ① Agathla Peak in Arizona is a plug of an old volcano. Dykes cut across the volcano's rocks, and sills were forced between its layers. Now all the soft rocks of the cone have been worn away, and the volcano's plumbing is left bare as this spectacular mountain. The shading gives an idea of what the original volcano looked like.

Dykes and sills

Plug

Original volcano

▼▶ ② The Le Puy region of southern France has many volcanic plugs that have worn down more slowly than the land around them. These pictures show a church built on a small plug and a castle built on a larger one.

▶ ③ The upper drawing is a side view of what it might have looked like in the region of Edinburgh about 340 million years ago when volcanoes were erupting all around. The lower side view is what the landscape looks like today, and shows the position of some important buildings.

The Castle Rock volcano probably spurted lumps of congealed magma that flew through the air as cinders and volcanic bombs (see page 17) building up a type of volcanic cone called a cinder cone, while the Arthur's Seat volcano was bigger and its explosive eruptions produced mainly ash (page 17). Magma flowed through the cone to produce sheets of rock that now make the sill called Salisbury Crags. The surrounding landscape was also covered with sheets of lava. Not all of these events happened at the same time.

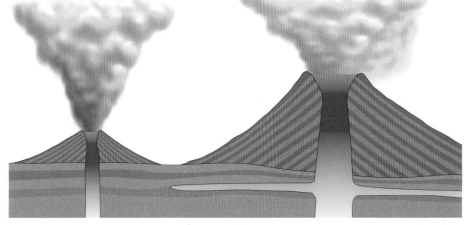

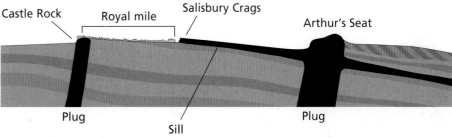

Castle Rock — Royal mile — Salisbury Crags — Arthur's Seat — Plug — Sill — Plug

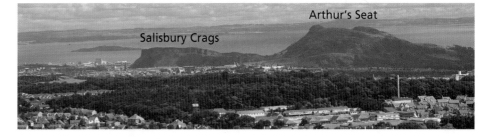

Salisbury Crags — Arthur's Seat

Crater lakes

Crater lakes tell of volcanoes that once nearly blew themselves apart.

Some volcanoes do not rise gracefully to a tall cone containing a small crater at the summit. Instead, they are more dumpy in shape. That is because the top of the cone is missing. These volcanoes often contain a large lake, called a **CRATER LAKE**. It tells of the most violent eruption that can affect any volcano.

How crater lakes form

The pit in which you find a crater lake has formed in a different way from an ordinary crater. To make a pit so large, the top of the cone has to collapse back in on itself. So while a crater is simply the top of a vent, a crater lake represents the collapsed top of the whole volcano.

To make a crater lake, the magma chamber feeding the volcano has to be quite close to the surface (picture ①). Then earthquakes can make the rocks above it crack and weaken.

During an eruption, some of the contents of the magma chamber are used up, so the chamber is partly empty. Above it lies the weakened rock, and on top of that is the immense weight of the volcano.

The weight of the volcano can be enough to cause the whole centre of the mountain to collapse down into the empty chamber below.

After the eruption is over, all that is left of the top of the mountain is a huge pit (which geologists call a **CALDERA**). In time it fills with water to make a crater lake.

▼ ① How a crater lake forms.

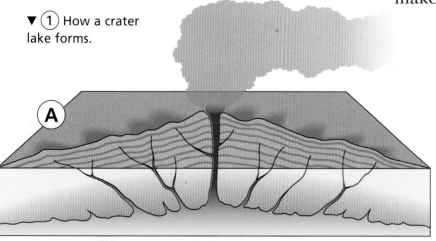

The volcano erupts violently, so that the rocks are weakened (A). At the same time, the lava pours out of the vent so fast that the magma chamber is left partly empty.

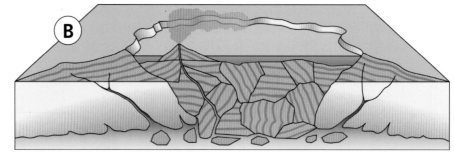

The weight of the volcano's cone makes it collapse in on the magma chamber, producing a vast pit that can then, over the following centuries, fill with water (B).

▲ ② This is Crater Lake in Oregon, United States, probably the world's most famous crater lake. The volcano used to be 4,500m tall, but 6,500 years ago the summit collapsed. The rim of Crater Lake is now about 2,000m above sea level, so more than half the mountain has sunk into the ground. A new cone has been building since this time. It forms Wizard Island in the middle of this picture.

One of the most famous crater lakes is in the state of Oregon, in the United States (pictures ② and ③). The volcano is called Mt Mazama. The lake in the summit is called Crater Lake. The lake is 11km across and the water is over 600m deep.

Just because the centre of the volcano collapses does not necessarily mean the volcano becomes extinct. Far from it. In the case of Crater Lake, a new cone is already forming above the surface of the lake.

▼ ③ This is Crater Lake from above. You can see the caldera very clearly and the flanks of the volcano picked out by snow. Wizard Island is near the back of the lake.

Geysers

Geysers are evidence that hot volcanic rocks are not far below the surface.

GEYSERS are natural springs that regularly send powerful jets of steam and water into the air (picture ①). They are found in places where rocks quite close to the surface have been heated. Many geysers therefore are found in the same areas as volcanoes, or where volcanoes were once active.

Hot rocks are also places where great chemical changes occur. As the hot water comes to the surface, it cools, depositing the minerals it contains on the land around, and building up the nozzles of the geysers.

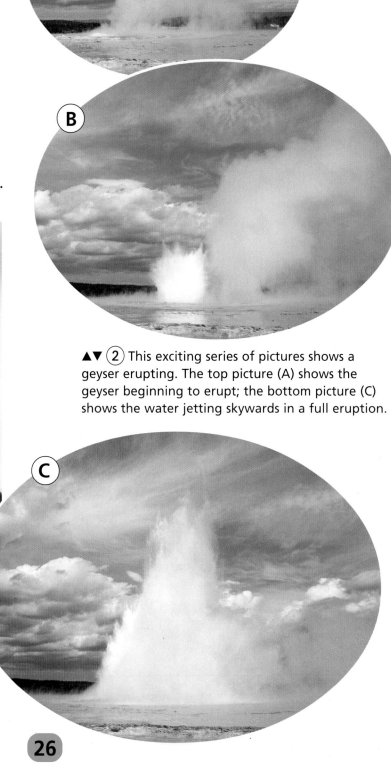

▲▼ ② This exciting series of pictures shows a geyser erupting. The top picture (A) shows the geyser beginning to erupt; the bottom picture (C) shows the water jetting skywards in a full eruption.

▲ ① This is Old Faithful, one of the most reliable and largest geysers in Yellowstone National Park, Wyoming, USA.

▶ ③ This diagram shows you the underground plumbing of a geyser.

Geysers in action

You know *where* a geyser will erupt because there is a hole in the ground or a raised nozzle, called a cone, through which it will spurt. However, because the geyser's 'plumbing' is hidden deep below the surface, it is very difficult to tell *when* a geyser will erupt. That makes geyser watching exciting (pictures ② and ③).

The first signs

When a geyser erupts, it begins by sending small spurts of water into the air, rather like a pan of water that is about to boil over. Gradually, the spurts of boiling water get more powerful and rise higher and higher, but there is always a pause between each one.

The main pulse

No one knows just how high the geyser will reach each time, but some of the world's biggest geysers regularly create fountains over 50m high.

As the pulses of water get stronger, and the geyser gets close to its main eruption, the gap between the pulses gets shorter. As the water fountain gets higher, it gets caught by the wind and a spray starts to float in the air.

After the main burst, the geyser collapses and the water flow ceases – until the next time.

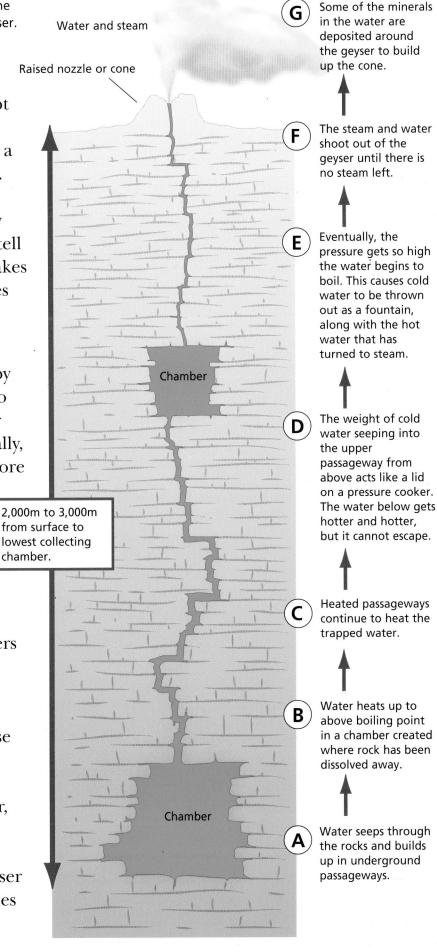

Water and steam

Raised nozzle or cone

2,000m to 3,000m from surface to lowest collecting chamber.

Chamber

Chamber

G Some of the minerals in the water are deposited around the geyser to build up the cone.

F The steam and water shoot out of the geyser until there is no steam left.

E Eventually, the pressure gets so high the water begins to boil. This causes cold water to be thrown out as a fountain, along with the hot water that has turned to steam.

D The weight of cold water seeping into the upper passageway from above acts like a lid on a pressure cooker. The water below gets hotter and hotter, but it cannot escape.

C Heated passageways continue to heat the trapped water.

B Water heats up to above boiling point in a chamber created where rock has been dissolved away.

A Water seeps through the rocks and builds up in underground passageways.

An earthquake strikes

An earthquake can come without warning and cause immense change.

▶ ① A picture taken during an earthquake. Notice the contents of the shelves have spilled over the floor.

An **EARTHQUAKE** is a very sudden, violent event. Unlike a volcano, which might begin to spout steam or give some other sign of being active, there is absolutely no warning before an earthquake.

An earthquake may last for half a minute, although it may seem like hours to those people who are close by (picture ①).

The Northridge earthquake

The Northridge earthquake struck the Californian city of Los Angeles at 4.30 a.m. on January 17, 1994. It was focused in the ground about 17km *below* the city of Northridge, just north of Los Angeles (picture ②). Geologists later reported it was a quake of magnitude 6.7 (see page 32).

The shaking rippled across 4,000 sq km of Los Angeles, but the main effects were felt at a place called Northridge, where the ground shook and heaved for twenty seconds. In that short time roadways collapsed, buildings fell apart,

and water, gas and electricity supplies were cut (pictures ② and ③).

Aftershocks

When an earthquake occurs, the stress disappears from the rocks that move; but places nearby that were not previously under stress may become stressed as a result. They, in turn, may fail, causing further earthquakes. This moving stress is the reason for the many smaller earthquakes (called **AFTERSHOCKS**) that are felt after a large earthquake. Aftershocks may occur for many years following a major event.

Cost

The main effect of the Northridge shock was to cause devastating damage rather than huge loss of life. This is typical of the way in which earthquakes affect modern industrial cities.

▼▶ ② The area near Northridge, Los Angeles. These pictures show how roadways collapsed.

Map of the Northridge area showing fault lines (see page 45).

Northridge

Los Angeles

The cost of repairs ran into tens of billions of dollars. Fifty-seven people were killed by the earthquake, and 9,000 were injured, a very small number compared to the area population of over fifteen million people. The numbers killed would be much higher in a poorer country where many people do not have the money to build earthquake-proof homes.

▲ ③ Balconies destroyed by the ground shaking.

29

What shock waves do

An earthquake is the result of a part of the Earth's crust snapping.

The crust of the Earth is always moving. Although the movement is very small – a centimetre or so a year – the crust is hard and brittle, and so it tends to move in small jerks rather than in a smooth way. Each jerk creates an earthquake.

Shock waves

Because the Earth's crust is brittle, when rocks near the surface are put under great pressure, they do not bend – they break. An earthquake is the pattern of vibrations in the Earth – called **SHOCK WAVES**, or **SEISMIC WAVES** – that occur when rocks break and move to a new position.

Rupture

The break that starts an earthquake begins at a single point and then runs along a line of weakness in the rocks like a piece of cloth being torn. The part of the crust that moves is called a **RUPTURE**.

The pattern of waves moves out like ripples moving outwards when a pebble is dropped into a pond of still water (picture ①).

The rupture extends itself, like a zip being undone, growing sideways and upwards at several kilometres per second. That only happens for a few seconds, but the results can be devastating.

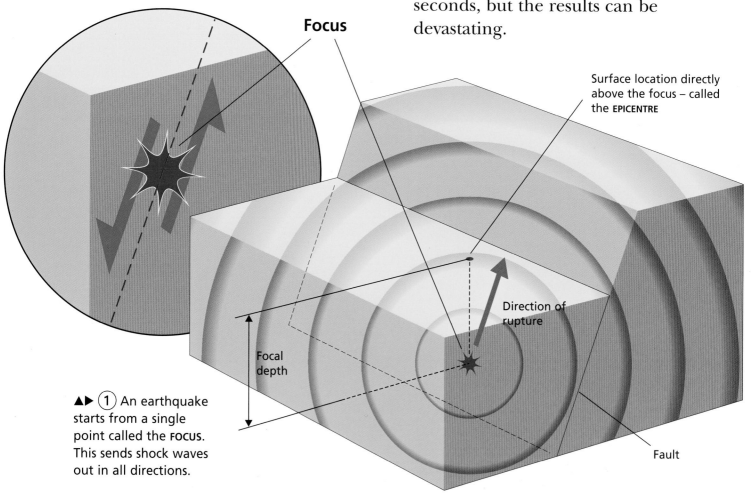

Focus

Surface location directly above the focus – called the **EPICENTRE**

Focal depth

Direction of rupture

Fault

▲▶ ① An earthquake starts from a single point called the **FOCUS**. This sends shock waves out in all directions.

Buildings
split apart

Buildings collide

◄ ② Buildings often show the way the ground is moving. If they are not strong enough, they will collapse.

▼ ③ During an earthquake these railway tracks were torn from their sleepers and refashioned into a wave. They show exactly how the ground moved during the earthquake. Different sections of track moved differently, showing that many kinds of wave occurred.

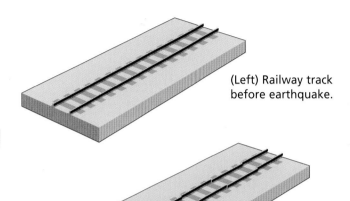

(Left) Railway track before earthquake.

Slow, damaging waves

Shock waves can actually be heard. It is sometimes possible to hear an earthquake as a deep rumble. But the waves that do the damage move too slowly to make sound waves. These slow waves can make the ground pitch and roll; and if this pitching and rolling lasts for long enough, cliffs will crumble, **LANDSLIDES** will occur and buildings will collapse (pictures ② and ③).

(Above) To-and-fro motion can cause a railway line to break.

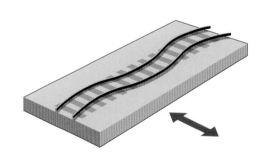

(Above) The sideways movement of some waves can also make the ground sway from side to side.

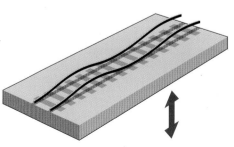

(Above) The effect of rolling surface waves can cause the tracks to buckle up.

Measuring an earthquake

The amount of energy in an earthquake is measured on the Richter scale.

The severity of an earthquake is actually hard to measure. Scientists know that the more energy released when rocks snap, the bigger the earthquake is. That is why they often use a scale called the **RICHTER SCALE** (pictures ①, ② and ③). On this scale each number is ten times bigger than its smaller neighbour. So a scale 4 earthquake is ten times bigger than a scale 3, and a scale 6 earthquake is 1,000 times bigger than a scale 3.

The world's most destructive earthquakes are, in general, scale 6 to 7.

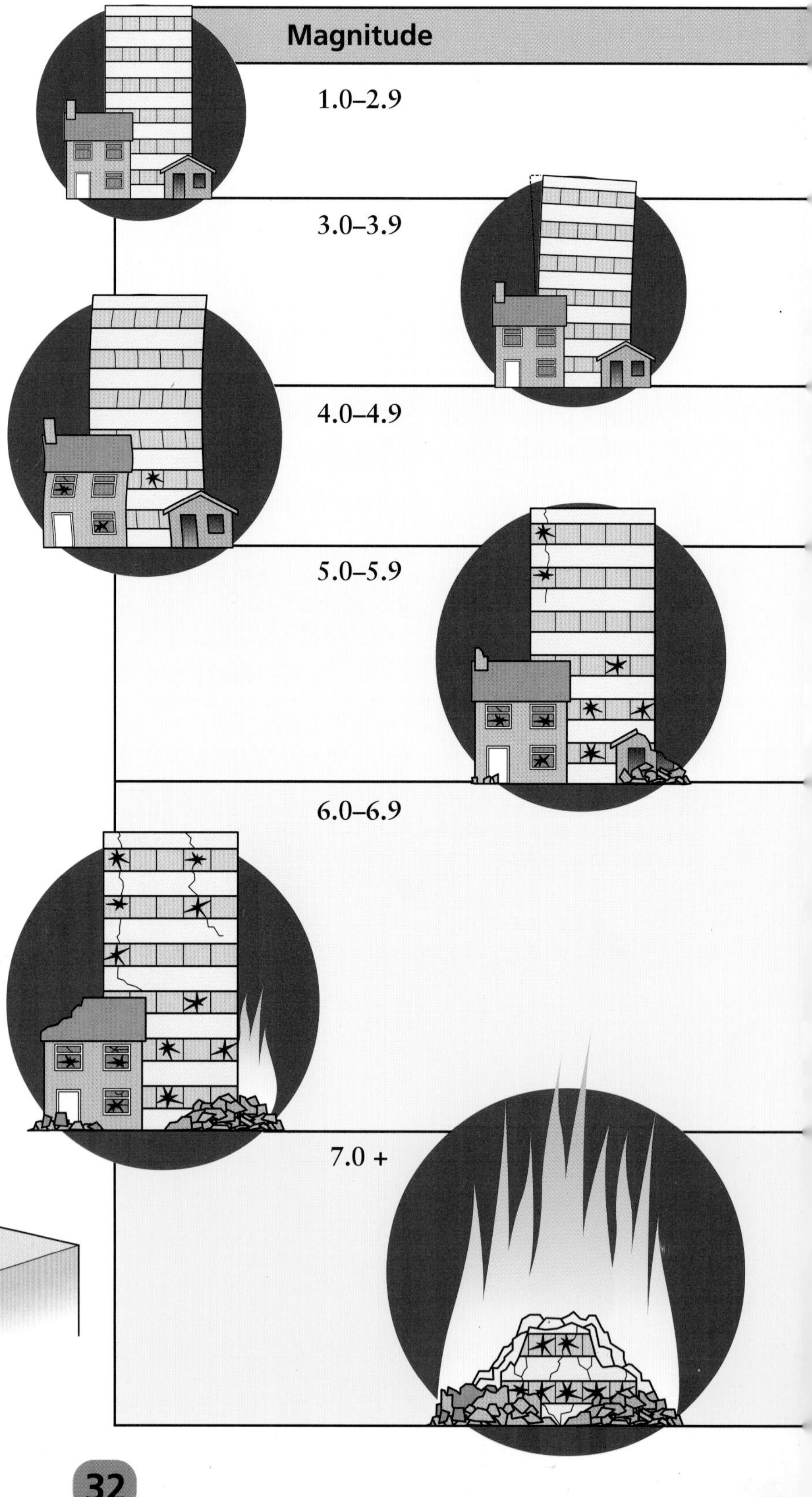

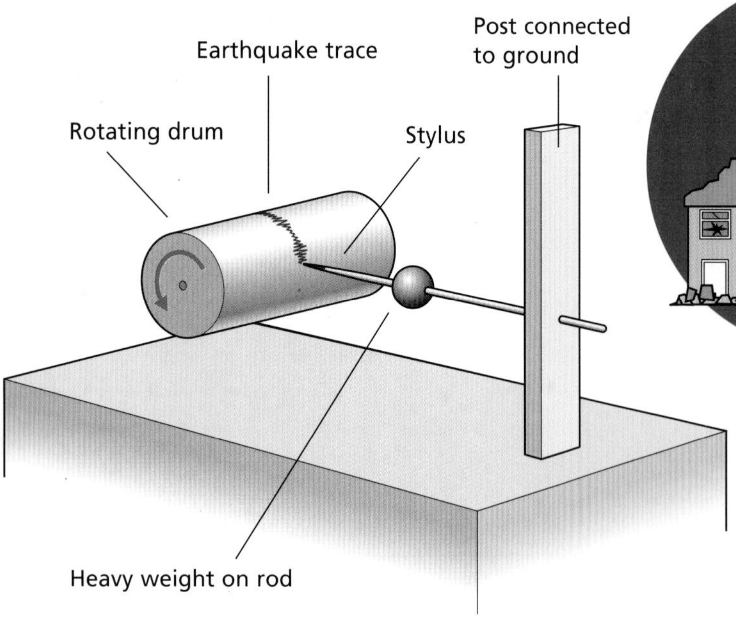

▼ ② A **SEISMOGRAPH** is an instrument that measures earthquakes. The design means that the drum will shake while the pen remains still. Since the drum also turns, a wave will be traced out on the paper.

Earthquake trace

Post connected to ground

Rotating drum

Stylus

Heavy weight on rod

▼ ① What the Richter scale means.

Magnitude
1.0–2.9
3.0–3.9
4.0–4.9
5.0–5.9
6.0–6.9
7.0 +

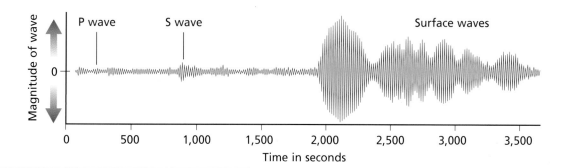

What happens
Hardly felt.
Felt quite noticeably by people indoors, especially on upper floors of buildings • Many people do not recognise it as an earthquake.
Felt indoors by many people • Quake reported on local news • At night people awakened by slight shaking motion • Some dishes and windows broken.
Many people will be frightened • Quake reported on national news • Plaster may fall from walls • Damage slight in well-designed buildings but considerable damage in poorly built or badly designed buildings • Some chimneys broken.
Many people very frightened • Quake reported in world news • Damage slight in well-designed structures • Considerable damage in ordinary buildings with partial collapse • Poorly built houses collapse entirely • Roads and railways buckle, gas and water pipes fracture, electricity lines torn apart • Fires widespread due to sparks from electricity cables while gas is leaking from pipes • Overhead roadways collapse • Major rescue efforts needed.
Few, if any, buildings remain standing • Bridges destroyed • Roads and railways buckle, gas and water pipes fracture, electricity lines torn apart • Fires widespread due to sparks from electricity cables while gas is leaking from pipes • Overhead roadways collapse • Objects thrown into the air • Widespread disaster often too large for a country to cope with on its own.

▲ ③ A typical earthquake readout trace, or **SEISMOGRAM**. The bigger the wave, the stronger the vibration. The first waves are small (called P waves and S waves on the trace). They hint at worse to come, but they give time to evacuate buildings. The main waves (called surface waves on the trace) are the ones that roll the ground about.

Earthquake effects

The amount of energy released during an earthquake is known, but the amount of damage it does varies considerably.

In an area where all of the buildings and bridges have been designed to stand up to an earthquake, even large earthquakes may not cause much damage. By contrast, the same size of earthquake in a place where the houses are not designed to stand up to an earthquake may result in total destruction and disaster. Thus, to some extent, people can affect how disastrous an earthquake is. They can either spend money on better designs before the quake and save lives, or they have to spend money rebuilding after the quake and many lost lives.

Weblink:www.CurriculumVisions.com/volcano

The Earth's moving crust

About 1,500 volcanoes have erupted in the last 10,000 years. Thousands of earthquakes take place every year. The places where they occur are very similar.

Volcanoes and earthquakes can be very puzzling features. Both volcanoes and earthquakes mainly occur in long, thin bands stretching across the face of the Earth. However, in some places earthquakes are found alone, and in other places only volcanoes occur.

Plates

Geologists have made some sense of this strange pattern by thinking of the Earth's crust as though it were a cracked shell, something like a hard-boiled eggshell that has been hit all over with a spoon. But in the case of the Earth there are just a dozen large pieces, and all of the pieces are on the move (picture ①).

Each of the pieces of the broken crust is known as a **PLATE**. Because each plate is moving, it can either crash into its neighbour, scrape alongside it or pull away from it. Plates that pull apart leave a great fissure through which magma can erupt quietly. In these places you can get volcanoes without earthquakes.

Plates that scrape alongside each other produce earthquakes but do not leave room for magma to rise and so do not cause volcanoes.

Plates that crash together buckle the rocks and produce *both* earthquakes and volcanoes (picture ②).

The volcanoes that erupt at this boundary are usually explosive.

Each slab is called a plate because it is a thin, curved sheet – like a dinner plate.

This is the African plate. The part of it above the sea we know as Africa.

The volcanoes that erupt at this boundary are usually explosive.

A plate contains both continent and ocean floor. This plate contains South America and also part of the Atlantic Ocean floor.

Volcanoes that form at this boundary under the sea are usually quiet and mostly erupt lava.

▲ ① A diagram that shows, in exaggerated form, the way the Earth's crust is broken into large plates.

▶ ② When slabs of brittle rock crush together, one slab often pushes below the other. The movement is a series of jerks, and each jerk produces an earthquake. That is why earthquakes are often connected to the boundaries between plates.

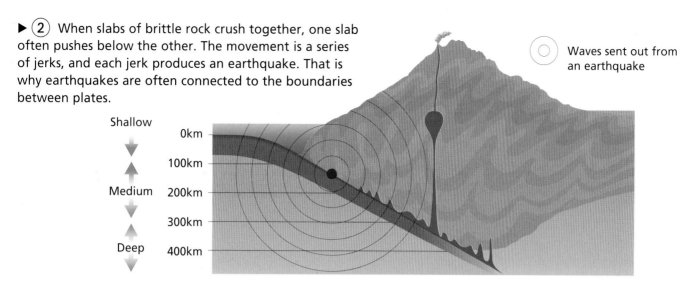

Waves sent out from an earthquake

Shallow

0km
100km
200km
300km
400km

Medium

Deep

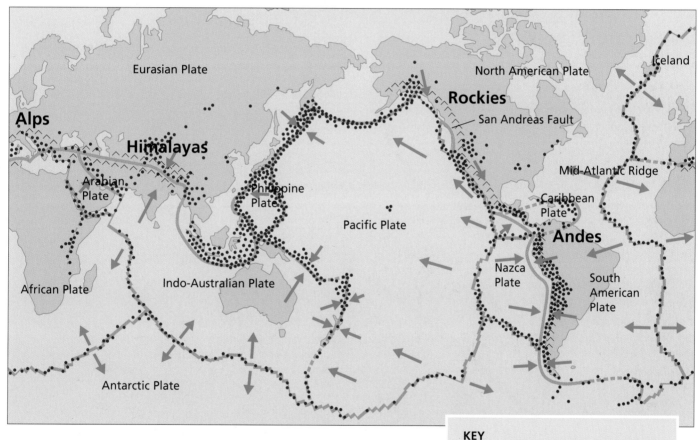

KEY

~~~ Plates splitting apart

— Plates colliding

^^^^ Fold mountain range

→ Direction of plate movement

• Recent earthquakes

When two plates collide, one plate is pushed down under the other, causing many earthquakes. Its rocks are heated and melt. The other plate is buckled up to make mountain **RANGES** and its rocks are weakened. As a result, the molten rock from below can rise up and make volcanoes in the plate above.

So, as you can see, by using the idea of moving plates, we can explain the pattern of almost all earthquakes and volcanoes (picture ③).

▲ ③ The Earth's crustal plates and major mountain ranges. The red dots show recent earthquakes which, like volcanoes, show where the plate boundaries are.

Weblink:www.CurriculumVisions.com/volcano

Inside the Earth

The crustal plates are dragged across the Earth's surface by moving molten rock below.

We can explain how the moving plates cause the pattern of earthquakes and volcanoes. But what makes the plates move? That is a hard question to answer because we cannot see the Earth below the crust. But geologists now think they know.

Convection currents

When a liquid is heated from below, it begins to churn over. This is known as **CONVECTION**. It happens in a saucepan of water on a stove, and it happens inside the Earth (picture ①), although on a very much bigger and slower scale.

Hot parts of the liquid are lighter than cold parts, and they rise, while cold parts sink. Between places of rising and sinking, rocks have to flow sideways. It is this sideways flow under the crust that pulls the plates apart in some places and makes them crash together in others.

From space it is often easy to see the plate edges, as shown in picture ②.

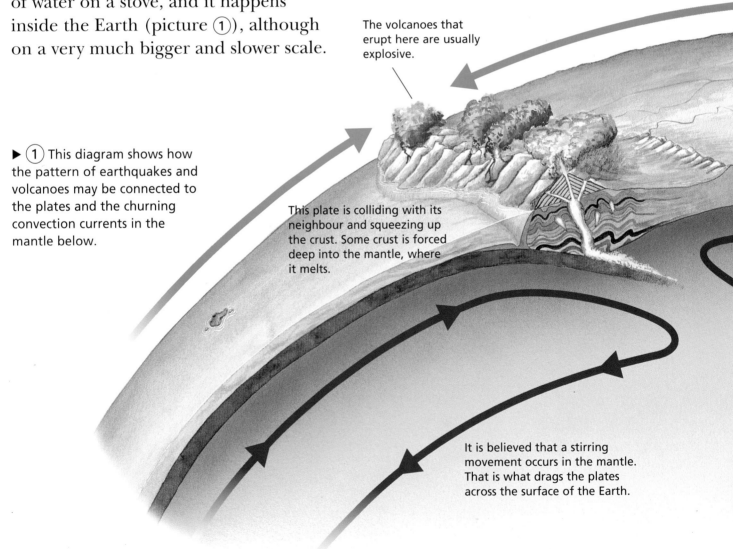

The volcanoes that erupt here are usually explosive.

▶ ① This diagram shows how the pattern of earthquakes and volcanoes may be connected to the plates and the churning convection currents in the mantle below.

This plate is colliding with its neighbour and squeezing up the crust. Some crust is forced deep into the mantle, where it melts.

It is believed that a stirring movement occurs in the mantle. That is what drags the plates across the surface of the Earth.

▼ ② The way the Earth works can often be seen more clearly from space than from the ground. This is a view looking west across the Himalayas, with the Tibetan Plateau on the right and the Ganges Valley on the left. The mountains mark the place where two great plates are crushing together. It is a place of many earthquakes and some volcanoes.

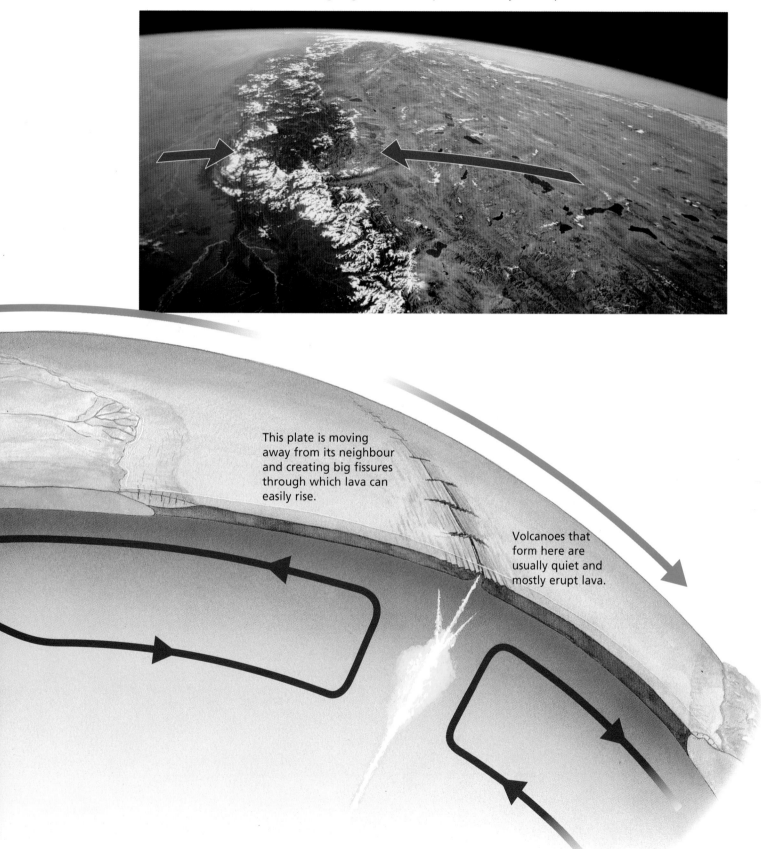

This plate is moving away from its neighbour and creating big fissures through which lava can easily rise.

Volcanoes that form here are usually quiet and mostly erupt lava.

Weblink:www.CurriculumVisions.com/volcano

Disasters caused by lava and ash

Volcanoes can cause an immense amount of destruction.

A disaster occurs when many people are killed and much property is destroyed by a natural event.

Many volcanoes make high mountains and few people live near their summits, so you might think they have little effect. But this is not true, for eruptions often melt the snow that covers their mountain tops, causing floods and mudflows that can reach people tens of kilometres away from the volcano (picture ①).

Some towns and cities are built on the lower slopes of volcanoes. Many more types of disasters can directly affect the people there: they can be killed by poisonous gases or by glowing avalanches that roll down the flanks of the volcano; their homes can be destroyed by lava flows and buried by ash or swept away by **LANDSLIDES** and **MUDFLOWS**.

One of the most famous disasters happened to the Roman town of Pompeii. It was buried in ash during an eruption of Mt Vesuvius in 79 AD. Nearby Herculaneum was destroyed by a mudflow.

▼ ① Some of the many ways that disasters can strike people who live near to volcanoes.

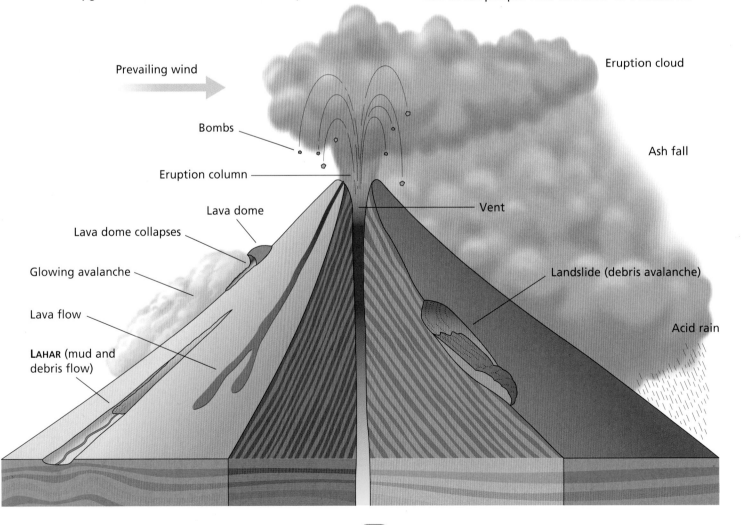

Prevailing wind

Bombs

Eruption column

Lava dome

Lava dome collapses

Glowing avalanche

Lava flow

LAHAR (mud and debris flow)

Vent

Eruption cloud

Ash fall

Landslide (debris avalanche)

Acid rain

▲ ② Lava sweeps across a road.

▲ ③ Lava destroys a forest.

Unstoppable lava

Tongues of lava on the move follow the shapes of the land, flowing down valleys and avoiding hills. Most people can therefore live in places that are not directly affected by lava. However, where people live on flat land, lava can spread over everything.

Lava flows rarely kill people because they have time to get away (pictures ②, ③ and ④). On one occasion in Hawaii there was even time to jack up an entire church and trundle it out of harm's way! But lava can destroy houses and farms, block roads, and in this way cause local disasters.

◄ ④ As lava reaches a house, the heat makes it burst into flames.

▲ ⑤ Ash blanketing cars after the Pinatubo eruption.

Destructive blasts

Explosive volcanoes commonly release searingly hot clouds of gas and ash. Sometime the clouds go upwards. Ash then falls from them and can smother the land (picture ⑤), bury crops and lead to famine.

If a gas cloud blows out sideways (picture ⑥ and pages 6 and 15), then people within the blast zone can be in great danger. It is unlikely they will get out of the way in time.

▲ ⑥ Whole forests knocked flat by a glowing avalanche (Mt St Helens, USA).

39

Disasters caused by earthquakes

Earthquakes can cause massive destruction, especially where the ground is not firm.

If an earthquake strikes a city, the scale of the disaster will depend on how well the buildings were built. It is likely that destruction will be worst in the poorer areas where people have not been able to afford to build to earthquake-proof rules. In a developing country, where the majority of people live in houses without strengthening, a disaster is therefore likely to be worse than for a similar-sized earthquake in a city in the developed world.

Unreinforced spells trouble

The houses most likely to cause deaths are those made of heavy brick or stone that has not been strengthened against earthquakes. People living in poor housing in the developing world are most at risk. Wooden houses may be damaged, but people inside them are much less likely to be hurt (picture ①).

Coping with recovery

The real problems will be fire caused by sparks igniting leaking gas and the fact that the shock will have left many people unable to help themselves

▼ ② In an earthquake, many children lose their parents, just as many parents lose their children. The survivors are usually very shocked and not able to help themselves for some time.

▲ ① After a strong earthquake, many people are left without homes for many months.

(pictures ② and ③). Disaster planning needs to concentrate on getting in teams from outside. For them to arrive quickly they will need to come in by air (picture ④).

▼ ③ Thousands of people may need temporary homes in tents. But in winter, tents can be bitterly cold to live in.

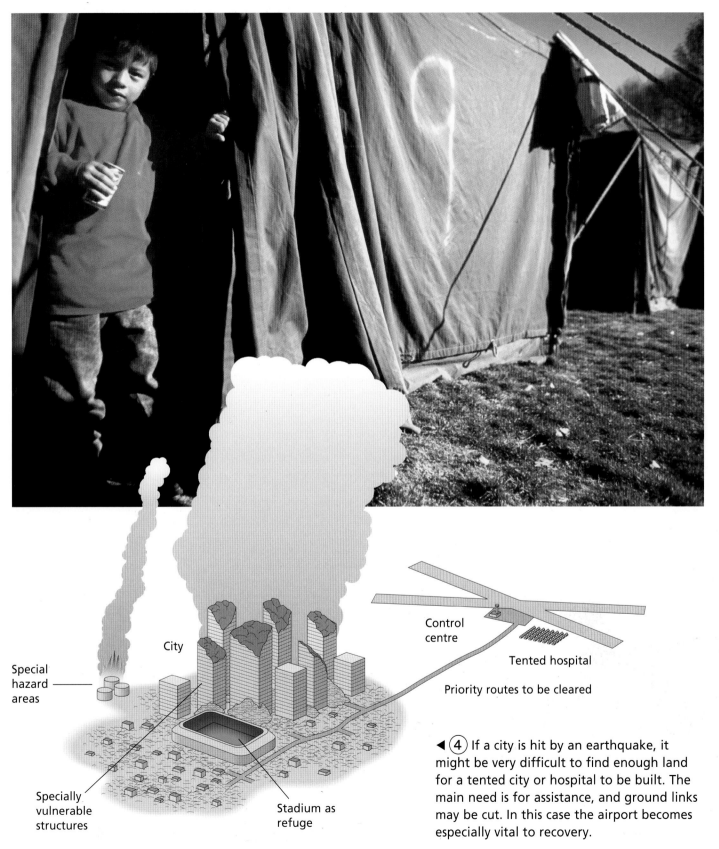

Special hazard areas

City

Specially vulnerable structures

Stadium as refuge

Control centre

Tented hospital

Priority routes to be cleared

◄ ④ If a city is hit by an earthquake, it might be very difficult to find enough land for a tented city or hospital to be built. The main need is for assistance, and ground links may be cut. In this case the airport becomes especially vital to recovery.

Weblink:www.CurriculumVisions.com/volcano

Places at special risk

There are certain places that are particularly at risk from earthquake damage. One of them is where the ground is soft.

Earthquakes do not have the same effect everywhere. There are places where the effects of an earthquake can be far more severe than elsewhere.

People who live on flat, hard rock are safest. On hillsides an earthquake is likely to shake the soil loose and start a landslide.

People who live on loose or soft ground are worst off (picture ①). The muddy marshes by a bay or river, the soft soil of a drained lake, or an area of land made by reclaiming the sea are all risky places to be in an earthquake.

Wobbling risk

Places with loose or soft soils are at risk because the soft soil makes the shock waves bigger. It is like being on a giant bowl of jelly. Even a slight shock causes the ground to shake.

Mexico City, which suffered terribly in 1985, is built entirely on the soft soils of an ancient lake bed. That is why in Mexico City many tall buildings rocked to and fro until they shook apart.

The bay area of San Francisco, California, has soft land just like Mexico City. That is why land by the bay suffers most during an earthquake.

Land that turns to quicksand

Waterlogged land can do more than shake. It can 'boil'. When this type of land begins to shake, the water inside it turns into something like quicksand. People see water bubbling out of the ground around them and then watch as their buildings silently sink into the ground. So a building that may have stood up to ground shaking falls down when the soil loses all of its strength.

▼ ① Mexico City was nowhere near the place where the ground ruptured. But it was built on soft ground, and when the shock waves reached it, the ground shook like a jelly.

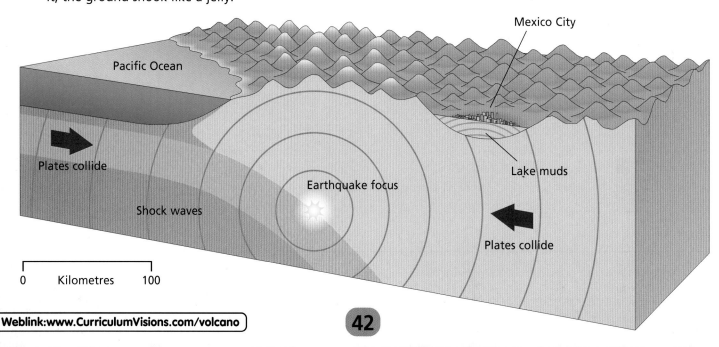

Pacific Ocean

Mexico City

Plates collide

Lake muds

Earthquake focus

Shock waves

Plates collide

0   Kilometres   100

Mexico Herald

Disaster! A day of misery, but it will come again...

Some buildings with weak floor-to-floor supports collapse like a pack of cards.

Some high-rise buildings simply shake apart.

It is an almost impossible task trying to rescue people.

It is a race against time to drag people from the ruins.

Only some buildings collapse. Those that were better built stay up.

Predicting eruptions and earthquakes

The world's active volcanoes are well known, but it is far from easy to say exactly when they will next erupt and what damage they will do.

It would be very nice if it were possible to predict exactly when eruptions and earthquakes would take place and where the danger areas lie. Unfortunately, most volcanoes and earthquakes do not give up their secrets that easily (picture ①).

Past eruptions

Areas that have been affected by lava and ash in the past will be the most likely areas to be affected in the future (pictures ② and ③).

But volcanoes can always burst out from unexpected places, as was the case with Mt St Helens in 1980, when a new eruption burst from the side of the old cone, not from the top as predicted.

Scientists know that valleys will be affected by floods and mudflows (called **LAHARS**) far more quickly than other areas, and so they must be evacuated first. Other areas at special risk are those that might be in the way of a blast of hot gas.

There may be an increase in the steam, smoke or gases.

Bulges may develop in the sides of the mountain.

▲ ① This diagram shows some of the signs that can be used to predict an eruption.

Earthquakes may increase in number, sending out shock waves.

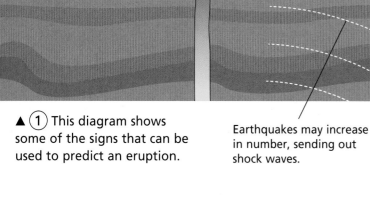

1924
1710
1890
1500
1945
1999
1990
1850

▶ ② By drawing maps of the land that has been covered by lava or ash in the past and the date it was covered, you can get some idea of what will happen in the future.

▼▶ (3) The Caribbean island of Montserrat experiences many eruptions, so a computer map was prepared to show which areas were most at risk. It was of vital help when the volcano erupted again in 1999. On the scale the red area will be affected first and the green last. Notice that valleys will be affected differently than mountainsides.

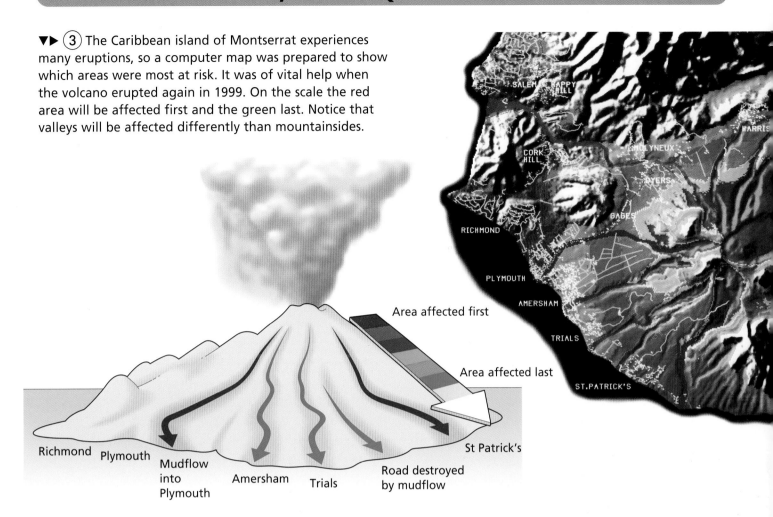

Area affected first

Area affected last

Richmond Plymouth Mudflow into Plymouth Amersham Trials Road destroyed by mudflow St Patrick's

Earthquakes

Earthquakes give no signs that they are about to happen. However, it is possible to map the lines of earthquakes because these lines – called FAULT lines – are the places most likely to slip in the future (picture (4)).

The rate of slip along the fault is also important. The whole of a fault does not slip at the same time. But, in time, each part must slip as much as its neighbours. By looking to see which parts of a fault have slipped recently and which have catching up to do, geologists can suggest where the next large, and possibly disastrous, earthquake is likely to occur. But they still have no clues as to when this might be.

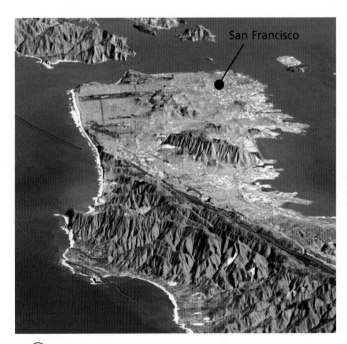

San Francisco

▲ (4) It is possible to see where the ground has ruptured in the past and so know which areas are especially at risk. This is a diagram showing the San Andreas and Hayward faults as red lines of weakness that pass through San Francisco (shown in grey).

Glossary

AA LAVA A type of lava with a broken, bouldery surface.

ACTIVE VOLCANO A volcano that has observable signs of activity, for example, periodic plumes of steam.

AFTERSHOCK An earthquake that follows the main shock. Major earthquakes are followed by a number of aftershocks that decrease in frequency with time.

ASH, VOLCANIC Fine, powdery material thrown out of a volcano.

BATHOLITH A very large body of rock that was injected deep into the Earth's crust and is now exposed by erosion.

CALDERA The collapsed cone of a volcano. It sometimes contains a crater lake.

CINDERS Pebble-sized lumps of rock that have cooled from magma while in the air. They have rough surfaces and look a bit like the cinders that remain after a coke fire.

CONE The name given to the shape of a volcanic mountain.

CONGEAL When a sticky substance changes from a liquid to a solid.

CONVECTION The slow overturning of a liquid or gas that is heated from below.

CORE The innermost part of the Earth. The Earth's core is very dense, rich in iron, partly molten, and the source of the Earth's magnetic field.

CRATER A pit at the top of a volcano.

CRATER LAKE A lake found inside a caldera.

CRUST The outermost layer of the Earth, typically 5km under the oceans and 50 to 100km thick under continents.

DISASTER A natural event that causes much loss of life or property damage.

DORMANT VOLCANO A volcano that shows no signs of activity, but that has been active in the recent past.

DYKE A wall-like sheet of igneous rock that cuts across the layers of the surrounding rocks.

EARTHQUAKE Shaking of the Earth's surface caused by a sudden movement of rock within the Earth.

EPICENTRE The place on the ground surface immediately above the focus of an earthquake.

ERODE, EROSION The twin processes of breaking down a rock (called weathering) and then removing the debris (called transporting).

ERUPTION The sudden outpouring of liquid and solid rock from a volcano.

FAULT A deep fracture or zone of fractures in rocks along which there has been displacement of one side relative to the other. It represents a weak point in the crust and upper mantle.

FISSURE A substantial crack in a rock.

FOCUS The origin of an earthquake.

GEYSER A fountain of hot water that rises periodically from rocks heated by dormant volcanoes.

GLOWING AVALANCHE A mixture of hot ash and gas blown sideways from a volcano during an eruption.

GRANITE A rock formed by the cooling of magma in a batholith. It is made of interlocking white, black and glassy-looking crystals.

IGNEOUS ROCK Rock formed by the solidification of magma. Igneous rocks include volcanic rocks, such as lava, and underground rocks, such as granite.

LAHAR A flood produced by a volcanic eruption, either by melting the ice from the cap of the volcano or through torrential rain. It brings very large amounts of mud (usually ash carried in water) with it.

LANDSLIDE A sudden slippage of soil and rock down a hillside.

LAVA Molten rock flowing across the surface of the Earth.

MAGMA The molten material that rises from the mantle into the crust and which sometimes reaches the surface. Once it has reached the surface it is described as lava, ash, cinders and bombs depending on whether it flows out of a volcano or is thrown out explosively. Most magma cools within the crust and becomes solid rock such as granite.

MAGMA CHAMBER A large cavity melted in the Earth's crust and filled with magma. Many magma chambers are plumes of magma that have melted their way from the mantle to the upper part of the crust. When a magma chamber is no longer supplied with molten magma, the magma solidifies to form a granite batholith.

MANTLE The layer of the Earth between the crust and the core. It is approximately 3,000 kilometres thick and is the largest of the Earth's major layers.

MOLTEN Turned into liquid.

MUDFLOW A sudden flow of mud and water down a hillside.

PAHOEHOE LAVA The name for a form of lava that has a smooth surface.

PLATE One of the great slabs of the outer part of the Earth. Plates cover the whole of the Earth's surface. The Earth's plates are separated by narrow zones of volcanic and earthquake activity.

PLUG The solidified core of an extinct volcano.

RANGE A long line of high mountains.

RICHTER SCALE The system used to measure the strength of an earthquake. Developed by Charles Richter, an American, in 1935.

RUPTURE The place over which an earthquake makes rocks move against one another.

SEISMIC WAVE A wave generated by an earthquake.

SEISMOGRAPH A machine designed to measure earthquake shock waves.

SEISMOGRAM A trace of an earthquake.

SHOCK WAVES The waves produced by an earthquake that shake the ground.

SILL A tabular, sheet-like body of intrusive igneous rock that has been injected between layers of sedimentary or metamorphic rock.

VENT The vertical pipe that allows the passage of magma through the centre of a volcano.

VOLCANIC BOMB A large piece of magma thrown out of a crater during an eruption. It solidifies as it travels through cool air.

VOLCANO (i) A mountain produced by many eruptions of lava and ash. (ii) An opening in the Earth's surface through which lava and ash can erupt.

Index

Bold page numbers point to the main entry/entries for a subject, italic page numbers show you where to find the definition of a word.